Pandas

James Maclaine

Designed by Amy Manning and Sam Whibley

Illustrated by Jenny Cooper and Richard Watson

Panda consultant: Professor David Macdonald CBE,
Wildlife Conservation Research Unit, Zoology Department, University of Oxford

Reading consultant: Alison Kelly

Contents

Panda bears

Pandas are bears that have black and white fur.

A panda has a large, round head.

It has black patches around its eyes.

It moves slowly on its short, fat legs.

A few pandas have brown and cream fur.

Panda homes

Pandas live in forests in high mountains in the west of China. Adult pandas live alone. They hardly ever see other pandas.

A panda finds part of a forest with plenty of trees and plants where it can hide.

Lots of bamboo plants grow in the forests. Pandas eat their tall stems and thin leaves.

Pandas live near rivers and streams so they can find water to drink.

Young pandas sometimes live together in the same place.

Bamboo eaters

Pandas spend a lot of time eating. They mostly eat bamboo.

A panda sits down and stretches out its back legs before it starts to eat.

First the panda eats the shoots and leaves of a bamboo plant.

Then it eats the stem. It has strong teeth that are good for chewing.

Pandas hold their food in their front paws.

This panda is
tearing strips
from a stem
of bamboo.

Sometimes pandas eat eggs, fruit
and small animals such as rats too.

Smelly pandas

Pandas show other pandas where they live by marking trees and rocks with smells.

A panda makes smells under its tail and rubs them onto a tree trunk.

Then it scratches the trunk. This shows other pandas it has left its smell there.

A male panda does a handstand to mark a tree with its smelly pee too.

This panda is sniffing a tree to find out if another panda has been there.

Pandas also leave dung to mark where they live.

Winter time

In winter it gets very cold and snowy where pandas live.

This panda is playing on a snowy slope. Its thick fur helps to keep it warm.

In winter a panda rubs bamboo leaves to break off any ice so it can eat them.

When rivers and streams freeze a panda drinks by licking the snow.

Sometimes a panda curls up in a ball to keep warm against cold winds.

Finding a mate

Before adult pandas can have a baby, they need to find a mate.

A female panda makes noises and smells if she wants to attract a mate.

A male panda finds the female, but sometimes another male finds her too.

The male pandas might fight over the female. The winner gets to be her mate.

This male and female panda will stay together for a little while before the male leaves.

In three to five months the female panda may have a baby.

Baby pandas

Baby pandas are called cubs. A mother panda has a cub every two to three years.

A panda makes a den inside a cave or hollow tree before she has her cub.

When a cub is born, it is very small. It has pink skin and hardly any fur.

The mother holds the cub close to keep it warm. The cub drinks her milk.

This cub is now six weeks old. Its black and white fur has started to grow.

Growing up

A mother panda takes care of her cub as it grows up.

A cub stays in the den for two months until it's big enough to go outside.

Then the mother and cub leave the den. She carries the cub in her mouth at first.

By the time the cub is five months old, it starts to walk by itself.

Panda cubs learn by copying their mothers.

This cub is
learning how to
eat bamboo.

A panda goes to live on its
own when it's about one
and a half years old.

Keeping clean

Pandas use their tongues, teeth and claws to keep their fur clean.

This panda is brushing its fur with one of its paws.

A panda licks its
body, face and
paws to wash
away dirt.

It chews its fur to
remove old hairs.
This stops its fur
from getting tangled.

A panda cub
doesn't clean itself.
The mother has to
lick its fur for it.

 If a panda's fur gets wet,
it shakes itself dry.

Climbing trees

Pandas are very good at climbing trees.

A panda wraps its arms
around a tree trunk
when it starts to climb.

It grips the bark with its
claws and pulls itself up
using its strong paws.

To get back to the
ground, the panda often
slides down head first.

This mother panda is teaching her cub how to climb a tree.

Playful pandas

Adult pandas and cubs both like to play.

Pandas slide down slopes and roll around on the ground.

A panda cub often climbs on its mother's back when it's playing.

A mother and cub also play-fight. They don't hurt each other.

Pandas in zoos like to play on slides and climbing frames.

Pandas sometimes
play in the branches
of trees too.

Sleep and rest

Pandas sleep or rest for several hours during the day and night.

This panda is resting in a tree.

A panda often lies on its tummy, side or back to sleep.

Sometimes a panda rests leaning against a tree trunk.

If it rains or snows, a panda might sleep under a rocky ledge.

A panda also rests in water to cool down when it's hot.

Panda cubs spend most of the day and night asleep as they grow.

Caring for pandas

There are fewer than 1,600 pandas living in the wild. Around 200 pandas live in zoos or sanctuaries too.

These young pandas live in a sanctuary where keepers take care of them.

If a panda is born in a zoo or sanctuary, the keepers help its mother to care for it.

 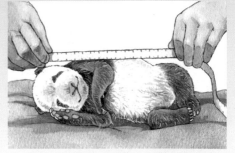

The cub is fed milk from a bottle several times a day.

The baby panda is measured to check how it's growing.

The cub sleeps in a heated box to keep it warm.

Born to be wild

Some experts train pandas born in sanctuaries to survive in the wild.

Pandas survive better if they aren't used to people. The experts wear costumes so they look like other pandas.

The experts show the pandas where to find bamboo they can eat.

They also teach the pandas to find places where they can sleep and drink.

When a panda has learned how to survive in the wild, it can live there on its own.

This is Xiang Xiang. He was the first panda to be set free into the wild in 2006.

Glossary

Here are some of the words in this book you might not know. This page tells you what they mean.

 bamboo - a plant with tall stems and thin leaves. Pandas eat bamboo.

 mark - to scratch or leave a smell. Pandas mark where they live.

 mate - an animal finds a mate to have babies.

 cub - a baby panda. Most mother pandas have one cub at a time.

 den - a place where an animal sleeps or has its babies.

 claw - a sharp, pointed nail on a panda's paw.

 sanctuary - a place where people take care of animals.

Websites to visit

You can visit some interesting websites to find out more about pandas.

To visit these websites, go to the Usborne Quicklinks Website at **www.usborne.com/quicklinks** Read the internet safety guidelines, and then type the keywords "**beginners pandas**".

The websites are regularly reviewed and the links in Usborne Quicklinks are updated. However, Usborne Publishing is not responsible, and does not accept liability, for the content or availability of any website other than its own. We recommend that children are supervised while on the internet.

This is a red panda. Although it's called a panda, it isn't related to the pandas in this book. It's much smaller and spends most of its time in trees.

Index

Acknowledgements

Photographic manipulation by John Russell

Photo credits

The publishers are grateful to the following for permission to reproduce material:
cover © **JOHN SHAW/SCIENCE PHOTO LIBRARY**; p1© **Lisa & Mike Husar/TeamHusar.com**;
p2-3 © **age footstock/age footstock/SuperStock**; p5 © **Heather Angel/Natural Visions**;
p7 © **Eric Baccega/naturepl.com**; p9 © **Lisa & Mike Husar/TeamHusar.com**; p10 © **Heather
Angel/Natural Visions**; p13 © **Craig Salvas**; p15 © **Lisa & Mike Husar/TeamHusar.com**; p17 ©
Alaska Stock - Design Pics/Alaska Stock - Design Pics/SuperStock; p18-19 © **age footstock
Spain, S.L./Alamy**; p21 © **Xinhua/Photoshot**; p23 © **Lisa & Mike Husar/TeamHusar.com**; p 24
© **Tom Walker/Getty Images**; p26 © **Koji Aoki/Aflo/Corbis**; p27 © **Gerry Ellis/Getty Images**;
p29 © **Gerry Ellis/Minden Pictures/FLPA**; p31© **M.Watson/ardea.com**

Every effort has been made to trace and acknowledge ownership of copyright. If any rights have
been omitted, the publishers offer to rectify this in any subsequent editions following notification.